www.ingramcontent.com/pod-product-compliance
Lightning Source LLC
Chambersburg PA
CBHW041710160426
43209CB00018B/1792

Copyright © 2025 Jennifer Jones
All copyright laws and rights reserved.
Published in the U.S.A.
For more information, email info@ninjalifehacks.tv
Paperback ISBN: 978-1-63731-957-4
Hardcover ISBN: 978-1-63731-959-8
eBook ISBN: 978-1-63731-958-1

Find the Turkeys on Strike lesson plans at ninjalifehacks.tv

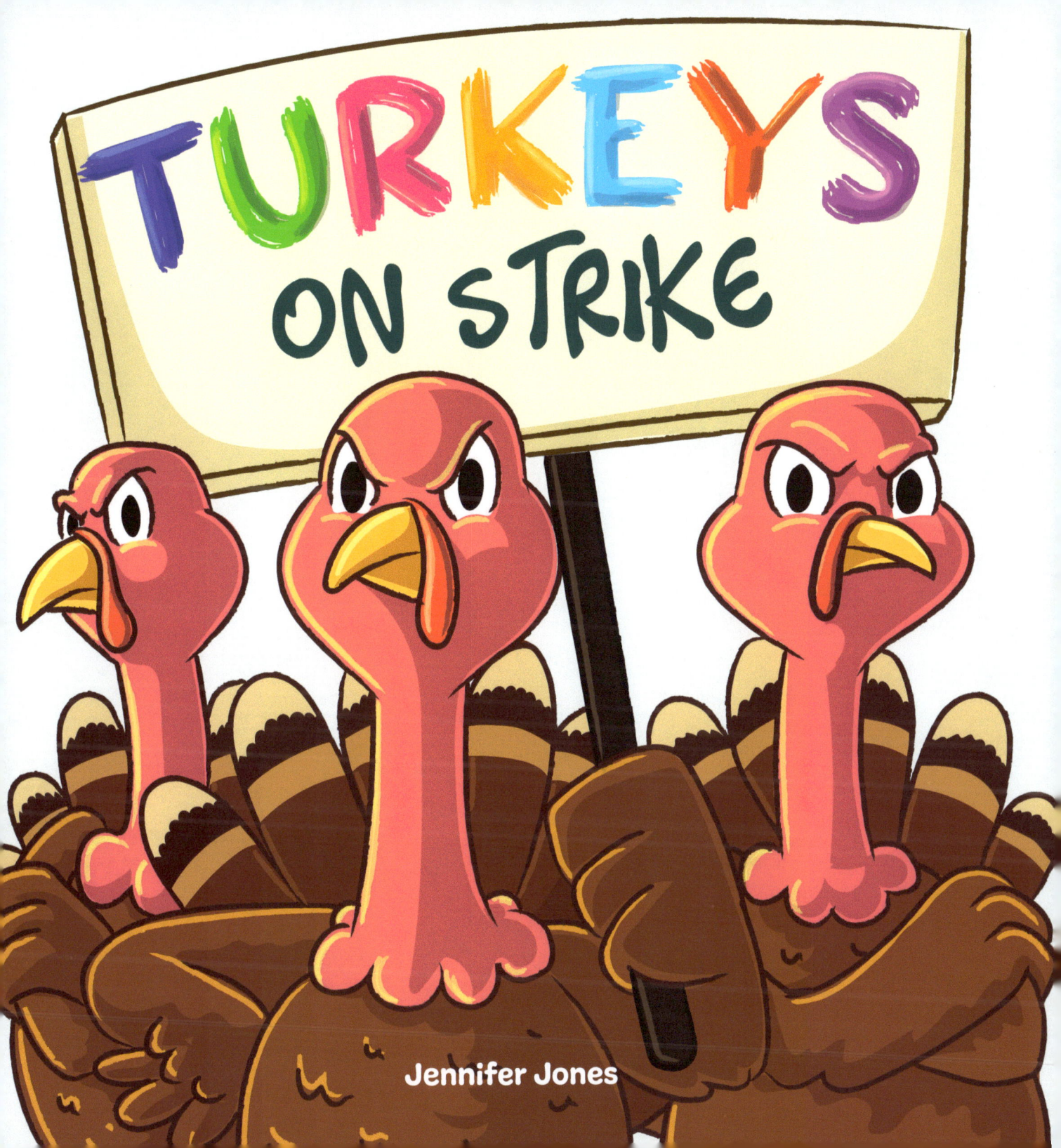

No gravy, wings, or turkey legs. The whole flock flew the coop! Instead, a note was left behind signed by the Feather Group.

"No roasting, basting, baking us.
We've got big dreams to chase!
We'd rather dance and tell some jokes
than end up on your plate!"

That morning, something strange appeared,
a letter, big and bold.
It had a feather for a stamp
and stories to be told.

They wrote kind notes with glitter pens and baked some corn-shaped cakes. They built a stage from lunch trays too with sparkly, feathered drapes!

The turkeys came with flair and skill.
They twirled and danced and sang.
One juggled yams on roller skates
while dodging a boomerang!

Now every year they all give thanks
with joy and extra pie.
The turkeys get to dance and laugh,
not wave the day goodbye!

Create Your Turkey Talent Show Act!

What would your turkey perform on stage?

My turkey's name: _____
Their talent: _____
What they're thankful for: _____
_____
_____
_____

Draw your turkey here!

www.ingramcontent.com/pod-product-compliance
Lightning Source LLC
Chambersburg PA
CBHW041711160426
43209CB00018B/1803